ISBN 978-0-365-07490-8
PIBN 11338522

S

S

rseries at
Deerfield, Ill.
hone *Deerfield 241*

FALL SPECIALS OF GOOD VALUES

PHLOX SPECIAL

. P. Struthers, Rheinlander, Mrs. enkins, Rosenberg, Widar, Wanais, Riverton Jewel, Henry Murger, ntonin Mercie and Franken's Glo-—2 each above ten varieties, $7.70 alue only $4.95; clumps $9.90

PEONY SPECIAL

lbert Crousse, Dr. Brettoneau, me. Geissler, Eugenie Verdier, me. Calot, Rubra Triumphans, ugustin D'Hour, Mme. D'Aremerg, Festiva Maxima, Queen Vicria and Canari, 1 each, clumps -12 eyes $16.75 value for $12.50; 5 eye divisions, $4.75

ee our Special Tulip Collections on pages 18-23

IOIS

Franken's Catalog of Hardy Perennials
Evergreens - Bulbs - Roots - Shrubs

Nurseries at Deerfield, Ill.
Phone Deerfield 241

FALL SPECIALS OF GOOD VALUES

PHLOX SPECIAL

R. P. Struthers, Rheinlander, Mrs. Jenkins, Rosenberg, Widar, Wanadis, Riverton Jewel, Henry Murger, Antonin Mercie and Franken's Glory—2 each above ten varieties, $7.70 value only $4.95; clumps $9.90

PEONY SPECIAL

Albert Crousse, Dr. Brettoneau, Mme. Geissler, Eugenie Verdier, Mme. Calot, Rubra Triumphans, Augustin D'Hour, Mme. D'Aremberg, Festiva Maxima, Queen Victoria and Canari, 1 each, clumps 8-12 eyes $16.75 value for $12.50; 3-5 eye divisions, $4.75

See our Special Tulip Collections on pages 18-23

Have your suburban home grounds landscaped complete

Nurseries at Deerfield, Ill.
Phone Deerfield 241

FALL SPECIALS OF GOOD VALUES

PHLOX SPECIAL

R. P. Struthers, Rheinlander, Mrs. Jenkins, Rosenberg, Widar, Wanadis, Riverton Jewel, Henry Murger, Antonin Mercie and Franken's Glory—2 each above ten varieties, $7.70 value only $4.95; clumps $9.90

PEONY SPECIAL

Albert Crousse, Dr. Brettoneau, Mme. Geissler, Eugenie Verdier, Mme. Calot, Rubra Triumphans, Augustin D'Hour, Mme. D'Aremberg, Festiva Maxima, Queen Victoria and Canari, 1 each, clumps 8-12 eyes $16.75 value for $12.50; 3-5 eye divisions, $4.75

See our Special Tulip Collections on pages 18-23

OUR grounds are open at all times, and we ask our friends and customers to call and visit us several times each season. We try to make our grounds interesting and educational. Our trial grounds have over three hundred varieties of Tulips and other Spring Flowering Bulbs. In our fields you will see more than a half million plants, growing for your use in development of your home grounds and surroundings.

Hardy Perennials

Perennials are becoming more popular each year, and by careful arrangement one can have a continuous season of bloom from early spring to freezing weather. We are endeavoring to have at our nursery, together with the Holland, French and Japan bulbs, of which we are dealers and importers, all material needed to develop as fine a garden as you could hope to attain.

We are listing for the first time many new varieties this season and have in our trial grounds many more which you are invited to observe from time to time. Visitors always welcome. Garden Clubs invited.

Our plants are grown in the open field, which assures you of the strongest and best plants obtainable.

Less than 5 add 10c extra	Height	Per 5	Per 25
Achillea (The Pearl). White; for cutting	24"	$1.00	$3.75
Aconitum, Fisherii (Monkshood). Large dark blue spikes.	36"	1.50	6.25
Agrostemma Alba (Mullein Pink). White blooms. June-July	24"	1.25	5.00
Coronaria. Rich crimson in abundance; long stems	24"	1.25	5.00
Anchusa Italica (Dropmore). Gentian-blue. June-Sept	48"	1.00	3.75
Anthemis Tinctoria (Marguerite). Golden yellow	18"	1.00	3.75
Aquilegia Canadensis. Red, yellow. For naturalizing	24"	1.00	3.75
Silver Queen. White; fine for shade and naturalizing	24"	1.00	3.75
Chrysantha. Yellow. May to June	36"	1.00	3.75
Coerulea. Rocky Mountain Columbine. Blue	18"	1.25	5.00
Long Spurred Hybrids. Assorted	36"	1.00	3.75
Mrs. Scott Elliott strain of hybrids	24"	1.25	5.00
Aster. Hardy, Novae Angliae. Lavender-blue	48"	1.25	5.00
Climax. Lavender-blue flowers. ½-in. diam. Aug	48"	1.25	5.00
Bocconia (Plume Poppy). Creamy-white; for massing	72"	1.00	3.75
Baptisca Australis. Dark blue; for wild border	36"	1.00	3.75
Boltonia Asteroides. White; for background. Aug.-Sept	72"	1.00	3.75
Pink. For background. Aug.-Sept	72"	1.00	3.75
Carnation Grenadin. Red, white, pink, brown. June-Sept.	12"	1.00	3.75
Campanula. Biennial; blue, lilac, pink and mixed	36"	1.00	3.75
Chrysanthemums. C. Lothian Bell. Large daisy-like; white	18"	1.00	3.75
King Edward. White, daisy-like flowers	36"	1.00	3.75
Centaurea, Montana (Corn Flower). Blue. July-Sept	24"	1.00	3.75
Coreopsis. Double-flowering, yellow. All summer	24"	1.00	3.75
Delphinium Belladonna. Sky-blue. June-Oct. For cutting	36"	1.00	3.75
Bellamosa. Deep blue. June-Oct. For cutting	36"	1.00	3.75
Chinese Blue. Blue. June-Oct. Border	24"	1.00	3.75
Chinese Alba. White. June-Oct. Border	24"	1.00	3.75
Blackmore and Langdon Hybrids	36"	1.25	5.00
Hybrids. Assorted	36"	1.00	3.75
Dianthus Barbatus (Sweet Williams). Mixed colors. Border	24"	1.00	3.75
Newport Pink. Salmon-pink. Border	24"	1.00	3.75
Dicentra (Bleeding Heart). An old-time favorite. May-June	24"	3.50	....
Digitalis. Pink, purple, orange, mixed. Biennial border	24"	1.00	3.75
Shirley. White to deep rose. June-July	48"	1.25	5.00
Funkia Coerulea (Plantain Lily). Blue. Border	24"	1.75	7.50
Undulata Variegata. Lavender. July-Aug	24"	2.50	...
Gaillardia. Brownish-red. All summer. Border, cutting	24"	1.00	3.75
Gypsophilia Paniculata (Baby's Breath). White; cutting	24"	1.00	3.75
Fl. Pl. Double-flowering white. Cutting	24"	1.00	3.75
Hibiscus. Giant red, white, pink. All summer. Border	60"	1.00	3.75
Hollyhocks. Double yellow, red, pink, salmon and white	72"	1.25	5.00
Single. Mixed	80"	1.00	3.75

Hemerocallis (Day Lilies)

Citrinna. Pure lemon-yellow	36"	2.25	10.00
Florham. Frilled soft yellow	36"	1.25	5.00
Gold Dust. Rich clear yellow	36"	1.25	5.00
Kwanso. Double deep orange, shaded crimson	36"	1.25	5.00
Orangeman. Light orange	18"	1.25	5.00
Souvereign. Soft chrome yellow, shaded brown inside	36"	1.25	5.00
Thunbergii. Clear lemon yellow	36"	1.25	5.00

AQUILEGIA (Columbine)

ONE of the most beautiful hardy perennials producing graceful flowers on 2-foot stems. One of the most important of our early hardy flowers and should be grown in quantity. Beauty of form and variety of Colors is the special feature.

CAMPANULA

FLOWERS are very large, in lovely shades of white, pink, blue and deep purple. Grows about 2 feet tall. Blooms June to August.

HRYSANTHEMUMS, KING EDWARD

THIS very attractive plant blooms freely and is useful for cutting. Grows from 3 to 4 feet tall. looms all summer.

COREOPSIS

ONE of the most popular hardy, yellow flowers. Begin to bloom early in June and are a mass of gold until frost. Grow to 3 feet tall.

DELPHINIUM

ONE of the most attractive garden flowers. Having a beautiful shade of blue and growing on tall stems. Grows 4 feet tall. Blooms from June to July.

DIANTHUS (Sweet William)

COLORS range from purest white to darkest red with an infinite number of combinations of colors. Grow from 1 to 2½ feet tall and bloom all summer.

Iris Germanica

We have in our trial grounds several choice and select varieties of Iris, recently imported, which we wish our customers to see this season. We are not listing these varieties, but prices will be furnished on request.

Extra strong plants at double the list price.

Less than 5 add 10c extra

	Height	Per 5	Per 25
Alcazar. S. light bluish-violet; F. deep, with bronze throat	24"	$3.00	....
Arnols. S. rosy-bronze; F. velvety purple	24"	1.50	$6.25
Albert Victor. S. soft blue; F. lavender	28"	1.25	5.00
Canary Bird. S. and F. canary yellow. Fragrant	24"	1.25	5.00
Caprice. Rosy-red, falls deeper. Handsome	24"	1.25	5.00
Celeste. S. and F. delicate azure blue	32"	1.25	5.00
Eldorado. S. bronze shaded yellow; F. violet purple	22"	1.50	6.25
Florentina Alba. S. and F. canary white, flushed lavender	27"	1.25	5.00
Fairy. S. and F. pure white, suffused with soft blue. Fragrant		1.25	5.00
Gertrude. S. and F. deep lavender blue. Fragrant	27"	1.25	5.00
Her Majesty. S. rose pink; F. deeper shade tinged crimson.	25"	1.25	5.00
Hector. S. soft clouded yellow; F. velvety crimson-black	26"	1.25	5.00
Iris King. S. clear yellow; F. rich maroon bordered yellow	27"	1.75	7.50
Jacquisiana. S. bright copper crimson; F. rich maroon	30"	2.50	11.25
James Boyd. S. incurved dome-shaped light blue; F. violet.		2.50	11.25
Kochii. S. and F. rich dark purple	24"	1.25	5.00
Lohengrin. S. and F. uniform shade of pink silvery mauve	28"	1.25	5.00
Loreley. S. light yellow; F. ultramarine blue, bordered cream	30"	1.25	5.00
Lygia. S. pale mauve; F. pale mauve, feathered dark mauve	26"	1.50	6.25
Ma Mie. S. and F. pure white with ruffled border, penciled blue		2.25	10.00
Madame Chereau. S. and F. pure white bordered clear blue	30"	1.25	5.00
Magnifica. S. light violet-blue; F. dark reddish violet. Large	44"	5.00	....
Mary Garden. S. pale yellow, flushed lavender; F. white	28"	2.00	8.75
Massasoit. S. and F. distinct shade metallic Venetian blue.	40"	2.50	11.25
Monsignor. S. rich satiny violet; F. velvety crimson purple	22"	1.25	5.00
Mrs. H. Darwin. S. and F. clear satiny white, base lavender	26"	1.50	6.25
Niebelungen. S. fawn-yellow; F. violet-purple with fawn edge	27"	1.50	6.25
Pallida Dalmatica. S. and F. immense clear light lavender blue		1.50	6.25
Pallida Odoratissima. Handsome fragrant flowers of light blue		1.50	6.25
Parc de Neuilly. S. and F. very dark navy-blue of reddish hue		2.50	11.25
Perfection. S. light blue; F. dark velvety violet-black	30"	1.50	6.25
Princess Victoria Louise. S. sulphur-yellow; F. rich plum.	27"	1.25	5.00
Prosper Laugier. S. fiery-bronze; F. velvety ruby-purple	25"	1.50	6.25
Purple King. Full rich purple; distinct and effective	30"	1.75	7.50
Queen Alexandra. S. fawn spotted lilac; F. lilac-bronze base	30"	1.75	7.50
Queen of May. S. and F. lovely soft rose-lilac, almost pink.	27"	1.25	5.00
Rheine Nixe. S. pure white; F. deep violet-blue	27"	1.50	6.25
Rose Unique. S. and F. deep violet-rose	26"	2.00	8.75
Seminole. S. soft violet-rose; F. rich velvety crimson	28"	5.00	22.25
Sherwin Wright. S. and F. rich golden-yellow; no markings	26"	1.25	5.00
Wyomissing. S. delicate pink; F. deeper pink shading to flesh	26"	4.00	17.50

Iris, Siberica

Siberica. Rich violet-blue	36"	1.25	5.00
Orientalis. Rich deep blue	36"	1.25	5.00
Snow Queen. Pure white	36"	1.25	5.00

Iris, Kaempferi. Japan Iris

Selected Separate Colors	36"	2.25	10.00
Fine Mixture	36"	1.75	7.50

Iris, Pseidacorus

Yellow Water Flag. Golden-yellow	36"	1.75	6.25

Intermediate Iris

Halfdan. Canary-yellow	21"	1.25	5.00
Prince Victor. S. blue; F. deep violet	24"	1.25	5.00
Walhalla. S. pale lavender-blue; F. wine red	21"	1.25	5.00

Dwarf Bearded Iris

Florida. Citron-yellow	12"	2.00	8.50
Pumila. S. violet-blue; F. deep violet-purple	12"	1.25	5.00

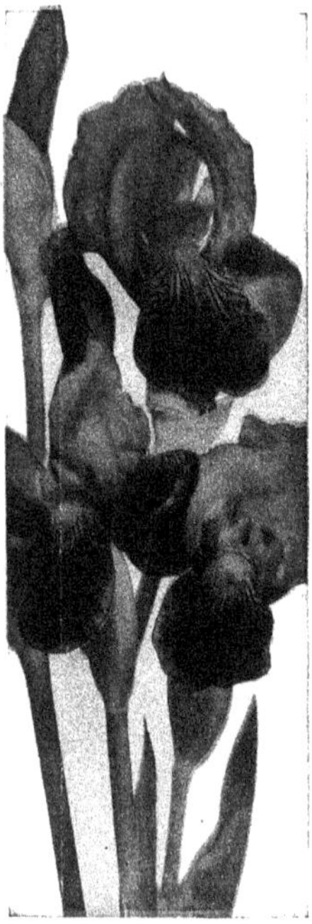

IRIS

THE German Iris is one of the most desirable early spring-flowering plants. Flowers of large size and exquisite Colors. Beautiful flowers that like the sunshine.

DIGITALIS (Foxglove)

TALL, dignified spikes of the Foxglove are always Charming. Colors are white, lilac, purple, rose and yellow. Blooms in June and July.

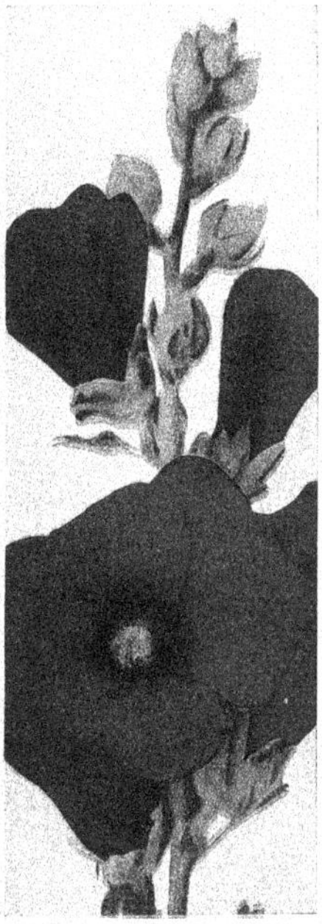

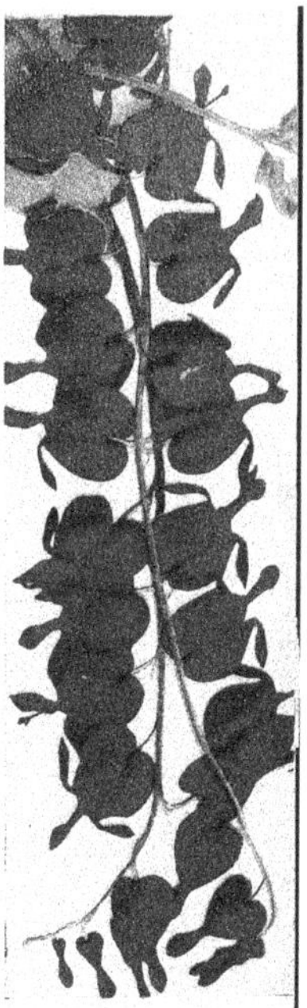

HARDY PINK

VERY desirable, sweet-scented, low-growing, early blooming and free-flowering. Many beautiful combinations of colors. Blooms in May.

GAILLARDIA

THESE deserve a place in all gardens. They are showy, bloom under adverse conditions and are easy of culture. Grow 2 feet tall. Bloom during the summer.

HOLLYHOCK

A CONSTANT blooming, old-fashioned garden favorite. This plant may be used in many useful and decorative ways. The double varieties will give a great deal of pleasure. A splendid assortment of colors. Grows from 5 to 8 feet tall.

BLEEDING HEART

A VERY attractive plant. Grows from 2 to 4 feet and spreads out almost the same distance. Blooms April to June.

Hardy Phlox

We have one of the largest fields of Phlox in the central states and we ask you to be sure to visit our nursery when the Phlox are in bloom.

These prices are for one or two-stem plants which have 3 to 5 eyes. If you wish three to four-stem undivided plants double the following prices.

Less than 5 add 10c extra	Height	Per 5	Per 25
Antonin Mercie. Grayish lilac, pure white center		$1.25	$5.00
B Comte. Dark velvety crimson		1.50	6.25
Eclaireau. Bright rosy-carmine		1.25	5.00
Elizabeth Campbell. Salmon-pink with light center		2.00	8.75
Europa. Pure white, crimson eye		1.25	5.00
Franken's Glory. Velvety crimson. Each $1.25		5.00	
Henry Murger. Purest white, with deep rose center		1.25	5.00
Jeanne D'Arc. Pure white		1.25	5.00
L'Evenement. Very soft, tender salmon-pink		1.25	5.00
Lummineaux. Soft rose with carmine blush center		1.25	5.00
Mme. P. Dutrie. Soft delicate orchid pink		2.00	8.75
Miss Lingard. Pure white with pale lilac eye		1.50	6.25
Mrs. Chas. Dorr. Solid blue mauve		1.25	5.00
Mrs. Jenkins. Purest white		1.25	5.00
Rheinlander. Salmon-pink with claret eye		1.50	6.25
Riverton Jewel. Mauve-rose with carmine eye		1.50	6.25
R. P. Struthers. Bright rosy red with crimson eye		1.50	6.25
Rosenberg. Rich carmine violet with blood red eye		1.25	5.00
Rhynstrom. Beautiful clear pink		1.50	6.25
Snowbird. Pure white, soft pink eye		1.25	5.00
Thor. Deep salmon-pink, with soft pink eye		1.50	6.25
Viking. Soft salmon-rose		1.50	6.25
Wanadis. Lilac blue, with reddish violet eye		1.25	5.00
Widar. Violet blue with pure white center		1.25	5.00
W. C. Egan. Delicate lilac pink with solferino eye		1.75	7.50

Other Splendid Hardy Perennials

	(inches)		
Lychnis Chalcedonia. Orange-scarlet. June-July	18"	1.00	3.75
Linum Perene (Flax). Blue; all summer; rockery	18"	1.00	3.75
Lupinus Polyphyllus. Pink, dark and light blue. May-July	30"	1.00	3.75
Poppy, Oriental. Scarlet. July. In shrubbery	24"	.25	5.00
Prince's Victoria Louise. Lilac rose	24"	1.25	5.00
Hybrids. Salmon shades	24"	1.25	5.00
Iceland. Single and double. Mixed	24"	1.00	3.75
Physotegia Virginica. Pink and white borders	48"	1.00	3.75
Platycodon. Blue and white Balloon Flower. Cutting, brdr.	24"	1.00	3.75
Pyrethrum Arto. Sanguineum	30"	1.00	3.75
Pyrethrum Roseum	30"	1.00	3.75
Rudbeckia Newmanii. Yellow Daisy-like flower	36"	1.00	3.75
Lacinata. (Golden-Glow). Yellow	60"	1.00	3.75
Purpurea (Cone Flower). Purple	36"	1.00	3.75
Scabiosa (Mourning Bride). Lavender-blue	24"	1.75	7.50
Sedum Spectibile. Light rose; July-Sept. Rockery, brdr.	12"	1.75	7.50
Brilliant. Red. Rockery, border	12"	1.75	7.50
Stokesia Cyanea (Speedwell). Lavender-blue. June-Sept.	18"	1.00	3.75
Veronica Longifolia Subsellis. Deep blue. July-Sept.		2.00	8.75
Wallflower. Golden-yellow; blooms all summer	18"	1.00	3.75
Yucca Filamentosa. Small size	72"	3.75	

Novelties and Specialties

		Each	Per 5
Tritoma (Red Hot Poker). A novelty plant	3-4'	$ .50	$2.00
		Per 25	Per 100
Hyacinth Candicans. Creamy bell-shaped flowers	2-3'	$2.75	$10.00

PHLOX

THESE beautiful flowers enliven the summer months with their brilliant colors. Grow from 1 to 3 feet tall. Two varieties, early blooming, from June to August, and late, from July to frost.

HIBISCUS (Mallow)

THESE bear the largest flowers of any of our perennials and present a gorgeous sight when in bloom. Grows 3 to 8 feet tall. Leaves large and grayish-green in color. Colors range from white to crimson. Blooms from July to September.

PLATYCODON

THESE form neat branched bushes of upright habit, 2 to 2½ feet high. Flowers are attractive lue or white from July to October. Deservedly ne of the most popular hardy plants.

RUDBECKIA (Golden Glow)

THE garden's gold is greatly enhanced in autumn by the sorts of Rudbeckia, especially the Golden Glow. Flowers produced in enormous quantities on long stems. One of the most popular. July to September.

PEONIES

THE Peony is a perennial that commends itself to you for many reasons. The blooms are beautiful and in their many tints of white, pink and red are a ceaseless delight to the lover of flowers.

PYRETHRUM

IN the form of a daisy these flowers are admired by all. The flowers bright in color are borne on long stems. Grows 2 to 3 feet tall. Blooms May to July.

Peonies

These prices are for strong three-year field-grown clumps, blooming size, with from 8 to 12 eyes. Standard size plants 2 to 3-eye. Divisions one-third these prices.

		Each	Per 5
Pink Varieties			
Albert Crousse. Very large, flat, compact bomb. Tall....	M	$1.75	$7.50
August Villumne. Rose type; dark violet rose; globular...	L	2.00	8.75
Chas. Leveque. Full compact, ball-shaped, salmon-rose...	L	1.25	5.00
Dr. Brettoneau. Pale lilac occasionally flecked crimson....	M	1.00	4.00
Delicatissima. Pale lilac-rose; fragrant, strong grower.....	M	1.00	4.00
Eugenie Verdier. Tall free-blooming; satiny sheen; delicate	M	1.75	7.50
Humei. Compact cherry-pink with silver tips. Fragrant..	L	1.00	4.00
La Tulipe. Semi-rose type; strong grower; free-bloomer...	M	1.75	7.50
L'Indispensible. Very large globe flower; light rose; late..	L	1.75	7.50
Livingston. Compact rose type, lilac-rose with silver tips..	L	2.25	10.00
La Rosiere. Semi-rose; several rows of white petals.......	M	1.75	7.50
Marie Crousse. Globular; uniform pale lilac-rose; strong...	M	2.00	8.75
Mme. Calot. Very large rose type; Hydrangea pink.......	E	1.00	4.00
Mme. Ducel. Light mauve-rose with silvery reflex........	M	1.75	7.50
Mme. Boulanger. Rose, bordered silvery; free bloomer...	L	1.75	7.50
Mme. Forel. Very large violet-rose, silver tipped center...	L	1.50	7.00
Mme. Geissler. Globular imbricated rose type, silver tipped	M	2.00	8.75
Mons. Jules Elie. Very large high crown; pale lilac-rose...	E	2.25	10.00
Rheine Hortense. Flat, compact rose type; Hydrangea pink	M	2.00	8.75
Triomphe de Lille. Pale Hydrangea pink; violet shaped..	M	1.75	7.50
Souvenir de Universelle. Violet-rose; silvery reflexed.....	M	1.75	7.50
Red Varieties			
Agida. Good bright-red Peony for garden effect...........	L	1.25	5.00
Augusto Dessert. Cup-shaped flower; crimson-carmine....		25.00	....
Augustin d'Hour. Large medium, compact; silvery reflex.	E	1.75	7.50
Berloiz. Poppy-red; erect; excellent for landscape purposes.	M	1.75	7.50
Felix Crousse. Globular; brilliant red; fragrant; free bloomer	M	2.25	10.00
Mme. D'Aremberg. Brilliant crimson; one of the finest...	M	1.25	5.00
Meissonier. Medium sized; brilliant purple-red...........	M	1.25	5.00
Officinalis Rubra. Large globular; brilliant crimson......	E	2.50	11.25
President Garfield. Very attractive dark red; good bloomer	M	1.75	7.50
Rubra Triumphans. Large, loose, globular, semi-double..	M	1.25	5.00
Tenuifolia. Brilliant crimson; single flowers; large as rose..	E	5.00	22.50
White Varieties			
Canari. White tinted pale pink; fragrant center; amber....	M	1.00	4.00
Couronne D'Or. Semi-rose; white ring of yellow stamens..	L	1.75	7.50
Duke of Wellington. White guards, sulphur center, fragrant	M	1.00	4.00
Duchess de Nemours. Pure white crown, white collar....	E	1.00	4.00
Festiva Maxima. Globular rose type; very tall grower....	E	1.25	5.00
Marie Lemoine. Pure white; the best late white known...	L	2.25	10.00
Mme. de Verneville. Pure white, center blush to white...	E	1.50	6.25
Monsieur Dupont. Large rose type, milk-white center....	M	1.00	4.00
Queen Victoria. Milk-white guard, tinted flesh..........	M	1.00	4.00
Yellow Varieties			
Solfatare. Large, milk-white; guards sulphur.............	M	1.25	5.00
Japanese Varieties			
Appleblossom. Blush yellow in central filamental petals....		4.50	20.00
Dainty. Single row of pale pink petals with yellow stamens....		6.00	25.00
Delight. Single row of American Beauty red petals, center creamy		5.00	21.25
Flashlight. Light rose, center petals amber yellow, shaded pink		6.00	25.00
Maiden's Blush. Rose-pink petals with golden center.........		6.00	25.00
Mikado. Dark crimson with filamental petals, crimson edged..		4.00	17.50
Nishiki Noshotone. Blush pink, semi-double striped darker pink		5.00	21.00
Some Ganoke. Rosy-crimson petals, center golden lined.......		6.00	25.00
Tatsu Gashiro. Single row of rosy petals, center rose, tipped gold		6.00	25.00
Takaradama. Single row of pure white petals, center golden...		10.00	45.00

Rock Garden Plants

Alyssum Saxtile (Madwort). Yellow; double-flowering..............
Anthemis (Chamomile). Yellow..............
Aubretia Hybrids (Rock Cress). Various shades..............
Campanula (Canterbury Bells). Perennial variety; mixed..............
Dianthus Caessius (Cheddar Pink). Pink..............
Forget-me-nots. Pink and blue..............
Gypsophilia Repans (Baby's Breath). Double white flowering..............
Linum Perene (Flax). Blue..............
Oenothera Youngii (Evening Primrose). Yellow..............
Pansies, Swiss. Giant mixed colors..............
Phlox Sublata. Pink, lilac and white; creeping..............
Polemonium Repans (Jacob's Ladder). Blue. June-July..............
Primula (Primroses, Mixed). Various shades..............
Sedum (Stonecrop). Yellow and red; creeping..............
Silene Sbafta (Catch-fly). Blush pink..............
Tunica. Very fine hair-like foliage..............

Rock Garden Evergreens

	Height	Each	Per 5
Juniper Prostrate	8–10"	$ .80	$3.75
Juniper Pfitzer	8–10"	.80	3.75
Juniper Pfitzer	12–18"	3.00	13.75
Juniper Savins	8–10"	.80	3.75
Juniper Savins	12–18"	3.00	13.75
Mugho Pine	6–8"	.60	2.50
Mugho Pine	8–10"	1.85	8.75
Thuya Pyramidal	8–10"	.60	2.50
Thuya Pyramidal	18–24"	2.00	8.75
Picea (Black Hills Spruce)	18–24"	2.00	8.75
Tsuga Canadensis (Hemlock)	8–10"	1.00	4.50
Pinus Nigra (Austrian Pine)	8–10"	.50	2.25

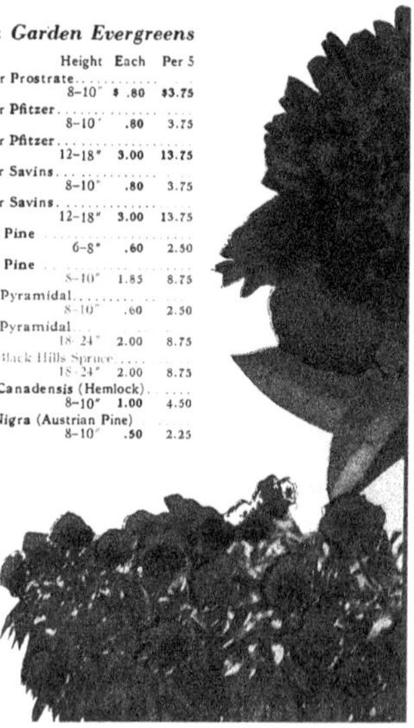

Gladiolus are valuable for House or Garden Decoration

Gladiolus

We have selected from one of the world's foremost growers of choice varieties a wide range of color and unique types to meet your demands.

Less than 25 add 10c extra

	Per 25	Per 100
America. Soft lavender pink	$1.00	$3.50
Alice Tiplady. A beautiful saffron-yellow	1.75	6.00
Baron J. Hulot	2.00	7.50
Evelyn Kirtland. Exquisite rosy-pink, shading to light pink	2.00	7.00
Gretchen Zang. Blooms of pink, blending to scarlet	1.75	6.00
Golden Measure. Golden-yellow; extra large flowers; tall	4.00	14.00
Glendale. Reddish-purple; tall grower	3.75	15.00
Joe Coleman. Purplish-red; ruffled petals	2.00	7.50
Lilac. Unique velvety violet. This new variety is very worthy of your consideration	5.00	.....
Louise. The showiest of all Gladiolus. Clear pure lavender with a blotch of velvety red towards center; large flower	2.25	8.00
Mrs. Francis King. Beautiful shade of flame pink flowers of giant size on tall growing spikes up to four feet with from eighteen to twenty flowers	1.75	6.00
Mrs. Frank Pendleton. A sensational beauty. Beautiful rose-pink on a pure white ground with deep velvety blood red blotch on lower petals	1.75	6.00
Myrtle. Beautiful pink; early flowering; of good size	2.00	7.00
Peace. Giant white flowered with lilac feathering in throat of two of the petals	1.25	4.00
Prince of Wales. Beautiful clear coral pink	1.75	6.50
Scarlet Precepts. Beautiful scarlet shade	2.25	8.00
Souvenir. A leading yellow variety	2.00	7.00
Assorted varieties of Hybrids or Primulinus	1.25	5.00

Roses

	Each	Per 10
Hardy Climbing Roses		
Dr. Van Fleet. Best pink climber in cultivation	$1.00	$9.00
Dorothy Perkins. Clear cherry-pink	.75	6.00
Excelsa Crimson. Blooms in great clusters	.90	7.50
Paul's Scarlet. Semi-double, purest red climber	1.00	9.00
Hybrid Tea Roses		
Gruss an Teplitz. Bright rich scarlet	1.00	9.00
Kaiserin Augusta Victoria. Largest best white rose	1.00	9.00
Lady Hillingdon. One of the leading yellow roses	1.00	9.00
Pink Radiance. Beautiful pink. Free bloomer	1.00	9.00
Hybrid Perpetuals		
General Jacqueminot. Greatest pink perpetual	.90	7.50
Paul Neyron. Clear pink blooms. Very fragrant	1.00	9.00
Rugosa Hybrids		
Conrad F. Meyer. Large double silvery rose. Fragrant	1.00	9.00
Grootendorst. Wonderful bright crimson	1.00	9.00
Rugosa Hansa. Very double; beautiful reddish violet	1.00	9.00

Hardy Climbing Vines

	Each	Per 10
Ampelopsis Engelmanii (Five-leaved Virginia Creeper). A hardy vine clinging to either brick or wood. Strong three-year plants	$ .60	$5.00
Ampelopsis Vetchei (Boston Ivy). Glossy green foliage, turns to crimson in the fall. Clings to brick or stone. Strong 2-year plants	.60	5.00
Clematis Paniculata (Sweet Autumn Clematis). Strong growing; small star-like flowers; delicately scented. Strong 2-year plants	.75	6.00
Wistaria Chinensis (Purple Wistaria). Rapid growing, with clusters of flowers from June to autumn. Strong 2-year plants	.75	6.00

Pink Radiance

Shrubs

	Height	Each	Per 10
Auralia Pentaphyllum (Japanese Five-leaved Auralia)	[illegible]	.85	$7.00
Auralia Spinosa (Devil's Walking Stick). Used where tropi-	2-3'	.9	8.00
cal effect is desired. Palm-like leaves	3-4'	1.25	10.00
Berberis Thunbergi. Neat and dense in growth; graceful	18-24"	.40	3.00
drooping habit. Leaves scarlet in fall	24-30"	.50	4.50
Buddleia Magnifica (Butterfly Bush). Reddish-violet	24-36"	.50	4.50
Cornus Lutea (Yellow Dogwood). Yellow in winter. Effec-	18-24"	.60	5.00
tive planted with Red Dogwood	24-36"	1.00	8.50
Cornus Siberica (Red Dogwood). Best variety on account	24-36"	.50	4.00
of its branches being showy in winter	36-48"	.75	6.00
Forsythia Intermedite (Golden Bell). The earliest flower-	24-36"	.50	4.00
ing shrub. Great profusion of bell-shaped yellow flowers	36-48"	.60	5.00
appearing before the leaves	48-60"	.80	7.00
Hibiscus (Althea). Lady Stanley; white crimson center	18-24"	.75	6.00
Hydrangea Arborescens Grandiflora. Blooms in July	15-18"	.60	5.00
Hydrangea P. G. Blooms in Aug. and Sept. when very few	18-24"	.60	5.00
shrubs are in flower	24-36"	.75	6.50
Lilac (Persian Purple). Lilac flowers in bread panicles	2-3'	.75	6.00
Lilac (Syringa Villosa). Late pink lilac from China	24-36"	.75	6.50
Lonicera Morrowi (White Honeysuckle). A bushy variety	36-48"	.75	6.00
of spreading habit; white and yellow flowers	48-60"	1.00	8.50
Lonicera Grand Rosea (Pink-Flowering Honeysuckle)	24-36"	.60	5.00
Philadelphus Coronarius (Garland Mock Orange)	36-48"	.75	6.00
Philadelphus Grandiflora (Scentless Mock Orange)	36-48"	.75	6.00
Philadelphus Virginalis. Semi-double; profuse bloomer	24-36"	1.25	10.00
Physocarpos Aurea (Golden Ninebark). Tall-growing va-			
riety with yellowish-white flowers; long stem	36-48"	.75	5.00
Prunus, Double Pink (Flowering Almond). Flowers in May	24-36"	1.25	10.00
Prunus, Pissardi (Purple-flowering Plum). Decorative	18-24"	.75	6.00
Prunus Triloba (Double Pink Flowering Plum). Like roses	24-36"	1.00	9.00
Rhus Typhina Lacinata (Fern-leafed Sumac). Tall grow-	24-36"	.60	5.00
ing fern-like leaves. Decorative fruit	36-48"	.80	7.00
Salix Discolor (Pussy Willow). Very interesting shrub used	36-48"	.60	5.00
for winter bouquets	48-60"	.75	6.00
Sambucus Aurea (Golden Elder). Golden-yellow foliage;	24-36"	.60	5.00
best when planted in bright sun	36-48"	.70	6.00
Spirea Anthony Waterer. Dwarf red-flowering Spirea	12-15"	.60	5.00
bright crimson flowers produced freely at intervals	15-18"	.70	6.00
Spirea Van Houteii (Bridal Wreath). Does well in all	36-48"	.50	4.00
locations. Weeping, graceful appearance	48-60"	.60	5.00
Symphoricarpos Racemosus (Snowberries). Ornamental	18-24"	.60	5.00
shrub: small pink flowers; has large white berries	24-36"	.70	6.00
Symphoricarpos Vulgaris (Indian Currant or Coralberry).			
Dwarf, compact habit; valuable for its red fruit covering	24-36"	.50	4.50
upper part of branches	36-48"	.60	5.00
Tamarix Pentandra. A new Tamarix recently introduced	24-36"	.60	5.00
Beautiful blue-green foliage	36-48"	.70	6.00
Viburnum Opulus (Highbush Cranberry). Ornamental on	18-24"	.60	5.00
account of its white berries	24-36"	.70	6.00
Weigela Desboisi. Rose colored; heavier than Rosea	24-36"	.60	5.00
Weigela Floribunda. Deep crimson; free-flowering. June	24-36"	.80	7.50
Weigela Rosea. Rose-colored Weigela; large sized shrub	24-36"	.60	5.00
in great profusion of flowers in June	36-48"	.70	6.00

Hedges

	Height	Per 10	Per 100
Ligustrum Privet (Amoor River North). Hardy growth.	18-24"	$2.50	$20.00
The best hedge for this locality	2-3'	3.00	25.00

HONEYSUCKLE (Pink Flowering)

A VERY popular Honeysuckle. Having beautiful pink flowers in May and producing a wealth of orange berries in summer. Grows 8 to 10 feet high.

SYRINGA (Mock Orange)

A TALL vigorous and hardy bush. In May it bears profuse white flowers resembling orange blossoms. Flowers are deliciously fragrant. One of the very best shrubs.

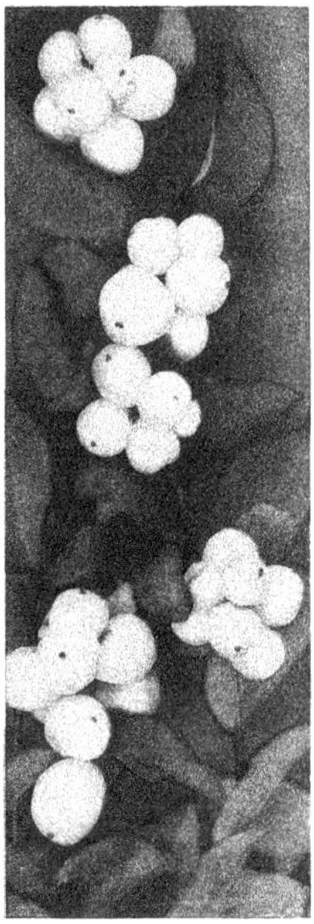

WEIGELIA ROSEA

ONE of the most popular and showy shrubs. Has numerous spreading branches that are covered with a wealth of bloom in June.

SNOWBERRY

ROSE-COLORED flowers in June and July, followed by large clusters of white berries that remain far into winter.

LILAC (Persian)

THIS splendid bush is loved for its pleasing fragrance and delicate coloring. There are a number of varieties to choose from. Colors, purple, white and reds.

FORSYTHIA

THESE beautiful bell-shaped flowers are borne in great profusion, the earliest of any in spring, and make a striking contrast on the bare landscape. Hardy and successful shrub.

Landscape Service

This group of illustrations is intended t and friends know that Franken Bros., Inc Landscape Service Department and we believ than we would be able to describe, the effici Service Department operates. Ask for estim

What This Means To You

Our Service Department is organized for those customers nee grading, preparation of the beds, laying out walks and drives, build seeding of lawns, are required.

It is just as important in planting the home grounds to have a landscape architect, as to have a plan for building a modern dwellin made by guesswork but are the result of careful study and thinking.

On orders amounting to $20.00 or more our Service Department and plant any stock listed in this catalog, at an additional charge o

Preparation of beds, fertilizer and black dirt, extra.

Evergreens: How and Where To Use Them

EVERGREENS properly placed and arranged add a charm and passing public an emblem of character of the home inside.

Those wishing to express these thoughts of loveliness and beauty i make no mistake by using evergreens.

Our Mr. Pottenger North Shore special ca terested in the Nursery a years. Knowing that e condition, he has work spraying, pruning, cult paring the beds before will blend well together.

The varieties we Landscape development been transplanted three making a root developm withstand the change c effect of having been m

Efficient Landscape adds Thousands to a Home

also lend

xecuted by Franken Bros., Inc., Landscape Service Department

Evergreens

Evergreens are for local trade only, as we do not ship them to distant points.

We deliver evergreens direct, as they must be handled promptly and carefully.

These prices are F. O. B. our nursery.

	Height	Each
Colorado Blue Spruce. Best known of all Spruces; light blue tipped. These trees make wonderful groups when planted three or more in a cluster. They should be planted far enough apart as they develop to large trees	2–3′	$10.00
	3–3½′	12.50
	3½–4′	17.00
	4–4½′	20.00
Koster's Blue Spruce. Selected grafted Colorado type	5–6′	50.00
Black Hills Spruce. Most compact of Evergreens and is recommended for screen or clump planting	2–3′	5.25
	3–4′	8.50
Pyramidal Arbor Vitae. Most popular and best of Arbor Vitaes. Grows very symmetrical in a pyramidal shape. Much hardier than other types	2–3′	5.25
	3–4′	8.50
Woodward Globe Arbor Vitae. Natural globe-shape	15–18″	3.25
American Arbor Vitae. This is the ordinary seedling type of Arbor Vitaes. Should be used where a cheap planting is a necessity as it is neither as hardy nor effective	24–36″	3.25
	3–4′	5.50
	4–5′	8.50
Concolor Fir. Without question the best of the Firs	3–3½′	8.00

Pyramidal Arbor Vitae

Evergreens carry their beauty and charm the year round and perhaps are even most appreciated in the winter, their warm foliage contrasts so sharply with the winter landscape.

Austrian Pine

	Height	Each
Douglas Fir. Most effective of the green type Firs. Transplants very easily and thrives well in shade. Used either in clump or screen planting	2–3′	$3.75
	3–4′	6.00
	4–5′	9.00
Juniper Virginiana. This is the common Red Cedar type Juniper. Should be used only where cheap planting is a necessity as it turns red in winter	2–3′	2.50
	3–4′	6.75
	4–5′	8.50
Juniper Virginiana Glauca. An improved type of grafted Juniper. Soft blue color; grows very compact when sheared annually. One of the very best Junipers	2–3′	6.50
	3–4′	8.00
	4–5′	10.00
Juniper Connarti. Another grafted type of Juniper. Much superior to its parent plants, the ordinary Cedars. Holds its color well throughout the winter; striking appearance	2–3′	6.25
	3–4′	8.00
	4–5′	9.50
Juniper Pfitzeriana. Without question the coming Juniper for natural landscape effect. For massing in beds	2–3′	8.25
	3–3½′	9.50
Juniper Columnaris. Also a grafted and improved type of Juniper introduced recently	3–4′	11.00
Junior Savins. This type of Juniper propagated by grafts. Very desirable for dwarf plantings	1½–2′	5.25
Juniper Tamariscifolia. Without question the most beautiful foliage of the Junipers when it thrives well	10–12″	2.75
	12–18″	3.75
Juniper Canadensis. An inexpensive dwarf Juniper. Looks very well in summer, but somewhat off color in winter	18–24″	2.75
	2–3′	4.75
Mugho Pine. This evergreen is without a rival for its green foliage and lasts the year around. Fine bedder	10–12″	3.25
	12–18″	6.00
Au trian Pine. This Pine may be used as a screen or clump planting	2–3′	4.50

Colorado Blue Spruce

Juniper Virginiana

American
Arbor Vitae
pictured
on the
right

A Planting of Various Evergreens is Distinctly Beautiful

All Bulbs Subject to

Fine Tulips

FRANKEN BROS. maintain a trial grounds for the benefit of their customers who wish to know and learn Tulips. Plan a day at Franken's during the blooming period this spring—you can then make selections and reservations for Direct Importation this coming fall. We have for years been closely associated with two of the best houses in Holland who pack your orders individually, especially for you, shipping to us in solid carload consignments, thus keeping the cost of importation to the minimum; in this way giving you the advantage of lower importation costs and enabling us to supply FRANKEN'S SUPERIOR QUALITY BULBS at truly reasonable prices.

More than a thousand people took advantage of this service last year and these people know exactly the color combinations, heights, how and where to plant these fine tulips at the time of ordering.

We want everyone receiving this catalog to take advantage of this service this season.

Plan a day at Franken's

A border of Hardy Bulbs

THIS picture illustrates the wonderful effect you can have with the use of Small Bulbs and Tulips listed in this catalog. Plan a spring garden for your own home grounds. Bulbs are very effective and dependable, and for an early spring flower they have no rival.

Plan to see our trial grounds this spring.

Lawn Grass Seeds, Fertilizer and Limestone

Less than 5 lbs. add 5c per lb.

Canadian Blue Grass	5 lbs.	**$1.30**
Kentucky Blue Grass	5 lbs.	**1.50**
Red Top	5 lbs.	**1.25**
U. S. Rye Grass	5 lbs.	**1.25**
Meadow Fescue	5 lbs.	**1.35**
Wood Meadow	5 lbs.	**3.50**
White Clover	5 lbs.	**3.00**
Mixture of above varieties in proper proportions to produce the best Lawn	5 lbs.	**1.75**
Vigro, the best Lawn Fertilizer	100 lbs.	**5.00**
High grade Calcium Limestone, to sweeten the soil (98.87% Calcium Carbonate)	100 lbs.	**1.25**

Market Price.

Fall Bulb Section

Chinodoxa (Glory of the Snow)

Dainty little star-shaped flowers blooming in clusters.	Per 25	Per 100
Lucillae. Beautiful blue with pure white center	$ .85	$3.20
Sardensis. Intense bright blue	.85	3.20

Crocus

A gay harbinger of the spring. Can be planted anywhere.

Albion. Lavender, striped white and violet	.80	2.75
Baron von Brunow. Dark blue	.80	2.75
Dandy. Blue, bordered white	.80	2.75
King of the Whites. Best and largest white	.80	2.75
Maximilian. Pure porcelain blue; largest of all	.80	2.75
President Lincoln. Large dark purple	.80	2.75
Sir Walter Scott. White, striped violet	.80	2.75
Mammoth Golden. The best and largest yellow	1.00	3.50
Crocus in fine mixture	.50	1.75

Eranthis

Early spring flower of bright yellow.

Hyemalis. Winter Aconite; yellow	.75	2.75

Galanthus (Snowdrops)

Dainty little bells that bloom in March.

Nivalis. Single white	.90	3.40
Nivalis Flore Plene. Double white	1.15	4.40

Muscari Grape Hyacinths

Dainty little bells resembling Lily of the Valley.

Heavenly Blue. Bright sky-blue	.75	2.80
Botryoides Album. Pure white	1.25	4.75
Plumosum (Feather Hyacinth.) Violet blue	2.00	

L'Innocence, La Victorie, Grand Maitre, Queen of the Pinks, and Gertrude Hyacinths

Emperor and Victoria Narcissus

Von Sion Narcissus

Scilla (Squills)

Early star effect flower with two or more spikes.	Per 25	Per 100
Campanulata Alba, Maxima. Large pure white	$ .80	$3.00
Blue Queen. Bright blue	.80	3.00
Rosy Queen. Soft lilac rose	1.25	4.00
Siberica. Sky-blue; mammoth bulbs	1.35	4.50
Alba. Pure white; mammoth bulbs	1.40	4.75

Freesias

Ilena. Deep rosy lavender and white	1.80	6.40
General Pershing. Pinkish-lavender suffused with bronze	1.50	5.00
Mrs. Marc Peters. Beautiful deep salmon	2.35	8.50
Purity. Mammoth pure white	1.40	4.60
Yellow Prince. Deep yellow; large open flowers	2.00	7.00

Narcissus or Daffodils

Emperor. Trumpet and perianth both yellow	3.75	14.50
Golden Spur. Trumpet and perianth both yellow; early	3.75	14.50
King Alfred. Rich chrome yellow; large	7.50	28.00
Sir Watkins. Golden cup and primrose perianth	3.75	14.50
Victoria. Creamy white perianth, fluted trumpet yellow	3.75	14.50
Von Sion. Double, deep yellow	3.50	13.50

Paper-white Narcissus

Paper-whites, Grandiflora. Extra selected	2.10	8.00
Grand Sol D'Or. The yellow Paper-white	3.75	14.50

Hyacinths

City of Haarlem. Pure yellow	5.50	20.00
La Victorie. Brilliant red	5.75	21.00
General De Wet. Light pink	5.75	21.00
Gertrude. Dark pink; large compact truss	5.75	21.00
Grand Maitre. Deep lavender blue	5.50	21.00
Lady Derby. Light rose pink. One of the finest	5.25	20.00
L'Innocence. Most popular pure white	5.50	21.00
Pearle. Brilliant sky-blue; large spiked; perfect shape	5.25	20.00
Queen of the Blues. Light porcelain blue	5.50	21.00
Queen of the Pink. Large truss; reliable	5.50	21.00
Bedding Hyacinths.		
Hyacinths, bedding, above varieties	4.00	15.00
Hyacinths, miniature, above varieties	2.75	10.00

FRANKEN BROTHERS have for years been importers and dealers in HOLLAND TULIP BULBS. Last year our sales of tulip bulbs were nearly double that of any previous season.

Prices are at the new low level this year and we are making contracts now for our next season's supply.

You will note many varieties as low as three dollars per hundred. We wish to advise early orders, preferably at our trial grounds where we have over three hundred varieties from which you may make your selection and at which time your orders will go to Holland and be packed direct by the growers themselves.

Darwin Tulips

*Tulips Marked (*) are good forcing varieties.

Pink Varieties

Less than 25 add 10c extra	Height	Per 25	Per 100
Afterglow. Bright orange lighter edge.		$1.80	$7.00
Barronne de la Tonnaye. Medium cup-shaped, bright rose	26"	1.00	3.50
*Centennaire. Violet rose-blue; base forcing or border	30"	1.00	3.50
Clara Butt. Clear pink, flushed salmon	21"	.85	3.00
Edmee. Beautiful cherry rose	30"	1.10	4.00
Flamingo. Soft shell-pink, medium pointed flowers	28"	1.35	5.00
Calathea. Bright carmine, rose-blue base; large flower	28"	1.35	5.00
*Mme. Krelage. Lilac-rose, inside soft pink; long flower	28"	1.00	3.50
Psyche. Silvery-rose inside, paler blue base; large flower	26"	1.00	3.50
*Princess Elizabeth. Deep pink; leading forcer	30"	1.00	3.50
Suson. Soft buff-rose, inside flesh-pink	25"	1.25	4.50

Red Varieties

*Barrigon. Fiery-crimson, white base; very showy flower	28"	.85	3.00
City of Haarlem. Dark scarlet-steel, blue base; cup-shaped	28"	3.25	12.00
Claude Gillot. Dazzling vermilion, white base, blue marks	25"	1.10	4.00
Europe. Salmon-scarlet, shaded rose with white base	22"	1.00	3.50
*Farncombe Sanders. Beautiful scarlet, white base		.85	3.00
Isis. Fiery-crimson, blue base; beautiful	26"	1.25	4.50
Ouida. Crimson-scarlet, purplish-blue base; huge flower	29"	1.10	4.00
*Prof. Rawenhoff. Deep cherry rose; large flower	24"	1.25	4.75
*Pride of Haarlem. Brilliant rosy-carmine, blue base; large	25"	1.00	3.50
President Taft. Dark red; splendid keeper.	30"	1.50	5.75

Violet and Purple Varieties

Andre Doria. Reddish-maroon with black base		1.50	5.75
Anton Mauve. Violet, bordered grayish-white. Plant in shade		1.60	6.00
Bleu Aimable. Bluish-heliotrope; late bloomer	26"	1.50	5.75
Dream. Pale heliotrope, inside deep violet	27"	1.10	4.00
*Euterpe. Silvery-mauve, edged paler lilac; long flower	28"	1.10	4.00
Faust. Dark satiny-purple, maroon blue base; large flower	32"	1.75	6.50
Jubilee. Bright blue-purple, paler edges, white base; huge	29"	2.75	10.00
*Phillippe de Commines. One of the best dark purples	26"	1.50	5.75
*Rev. Ewbank. Soft lavender-violet, darker toward base	22"	.85	3.00
Valentine. Soft heliotrope blue base; long; large flower	22"	1.25	4.50
Viking. Intense violet; wonderful keeper	26"	1.50	5.75
*Wm. Copeland. Rosy lilac, changing to lovely lavender	24"	1.10	4.00

Black Varieties

La Tulipe Noire. Dark maroon-black; large flower	25"	1.75	6.00
Zulu. Rich velvety purple-black, shiny purple edge	27"	1.10	4.00

White Varieties

Painted Lady. White, tinged heliotrope; good size	27"	1.00	3.60

Faust Farncomb Sanders Clara Butt

This collection of the beautiful Darwin Tulips, as

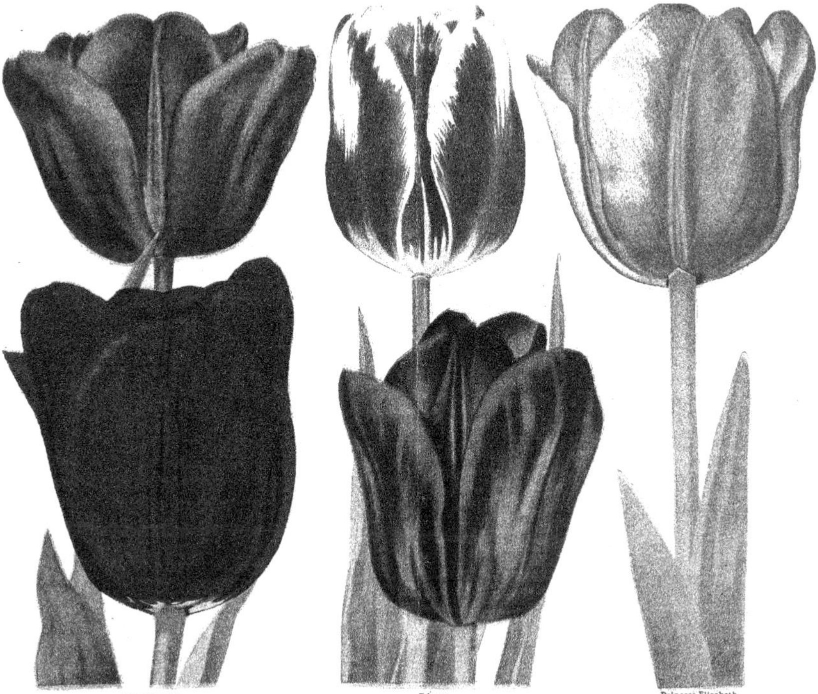

Blue Aimable
President Taft

Edmee
Phillippe de Commines

Princess Elizabeth

illustrated—25 of each packed separate—200 Tulips in all, only *$7.50*

Cottage Tulips

*Tulips marked (*) are good forcing varieties.

Less than 25 add 10% extra

Pink Varieties

	Height	Per 25	Per 100
Fairy Queen. Heliotrope, shaded yellow		1.10	4.00
Inglescombe Pink. Soft rosy-pink, salmon flush; large	24"	.85	3.00
The Fawn Pale. Rosy-fawn, flushed rose; large-egg shaped	20"	.85	3.00
John Ruskin. Salmon-rose, edged lemon-yellow; large	16"	1.25	4.50
Idyll. Lively rose, inside salmon-pink	20"	1.35	5.00
Kaleidoscope. Rose, striped mauve, yellow edged	20"	1.75	6.50
Marvel. Salmon, rose-yellow border, inside gold.	28"	5.50	22.00
Mrs. Kerrell. Rose flushed orange		2.00	7.50
Hammer Hales. Golden brown, flushed old rose, inside apricot		1.60	6.00

Scarlet Varieties

	Height	Per 25	Per 100
Coronation Scarlet. Orange shade; 3 to 5 flowers on stem		1.50	5.75
Dido. Orange-red, bordered orange-yellow		3.50	50.00
Dulcinea. Beautiful soft rosy-red		7.00	25.00
La Merveille. Orange scarlet, flushed rose-yellow base	20"	.85	3.00
Scarlet Emperor. Brilliant scarlet		1.60	6.00

Yellow Varieties

	Height	Per 25	Per 100
Avis Kennicott. Rich chrome-yellow, black base; large	25"	2.60	10.00
Bouron D'Or. Deep chrome-yellow; cup-shaped; medium size	18"	1.10	4.00
Gesneriana Lutea. Deep yellow; handsome growing among shrubs		.85	3.00
Golden Spire. Yellow, edged red		1.50	5.50
*Inglescombe Yellow. Canary-yellow; globe-shape	21"	1.00	3.60
Moonlight. Canary-yellow; large oval-shaped flower; superb		1.20	4.50
*Mrs. Moon. Golden-yellow; large flower; beautiful	25"	1.75	6.50
Orange King. Deep orange, shaded rose, yellow base; scented		1.00	3.80
Vittelina. Sulphur-yellow; large flower	24"	1.10	4.00

White Varieties

	Height	Per 25	Per 100
Picotee. Margined deep rose; good sized flower	20"	1.00	3.80

Single Early Tulips

	Height	Per 25	Per 100
*Belle Alliance. Scarlet; large sweet-scented	18"	1.25	4.80
*Flamingo. Carmine-rose, shaded lighter, white striped		1.25	4.80
*Fred Moore. Bright orange, shaded scarlet	16"	1.20	4.50
*Hobbema. Crushed strawberry; handsome; strong stem	24"	1.60	6.00
*King of the Yellow. Deep yellow; egg-shaped flower	20"	1.25	4.50
*Keizerkroon. Bright crimson-scarlet, edged yellow	16"	1.70	6.50
President Lincoln. Light violet with white base		1.50	5.50
Prosperine. Rosy-carmine, white base; scented; handsome	18"	1.70	6.50
Rising Sun. Deep yellow; very large flower		1.95	7.50

Double Early Tulips

	Height	Per 25	Per 100
*Couronne D'Or. Deep yellow, flushed orange red; large	11"	1.50	5.[illegible]0
*Imperator Rubrum. Glowing scarlet; popular. When forced let flower come slowly at first to prevent green tips	12"	1.70	6.50
*La Grandesse. Large soft rose, shaded white; good forcer	12"	1.25	4.80
Murillo. Delicate rose-pink, flushed white	11"	1.10	4.00

Miscellaneous Fruits

	Height	Each
Cherry, Early Richmond.	4-5'	$1.50
Concord Grapes	No. 1	.50

Moonlight
Scarlet Emperor

Orange King

This collection of Cottage Tulips as illustrated—25 of

Dulcinea
Mrs. Kerrell

Picotee
John Ruskin

Dido
Avis Kennicott

each packed separate—225 Tulips in all, only $25.00. (This collection includes some rare and expensive varieties.)

Breeder Tulips

Consists of a great many choice varieties on tall, sturdy stems, and a wider range of colors than the Darwin Tulips.

You will find in the breeders many choice colors of bronze, and many fair yellows, where there is neither of these colors found in the Darwins.

Breeders are very fine for rock gardens and plantings among evergreens. Many years have been devoted in breeding up this strain of Tulips from where their name, BREEDERS, has arrived.

*Tulips marked (*) are good forcing varieties.

Violet Varieties — *Less than 25 add 10c extra*

	Height	Per 25	Per 100
Bacchus. Dark violet-blue; best among dark breeders	28"	$2.60	$10.00
Cardinal Manning. Dull wine-red, flushed rosy-bronze	30"	1.25	4.75
Plutarchus. Dull-purple, inside lemon-yellow, green base	25"	1.50	5.80
Roi D'Siam. Light purple, lighter toward edges	32"	1.50	5.50
St. James. Dark rosy-lilac, edge bronze, inside mahogany	30"	1.60	6.00
Violet Queen. Ruby-violet; wonderful flower	30"	1.85	7.00
Velvet King. Dark glossy purple maroon, yellow base	25"	2.10	8.00

Yellow Varieties

	Height	Per 25	Per 100
Apricot. Flushed orange		1.80	7.00
Coridion. Clear yellow, lilac-striped through petals	24"	3.50	12.50
Lucifer. Dark orange, inside scarlet, orange-yellow base	28"	4.00	15.00
Marginata. Orange, shaded apricot, bordered yellow	30"	3.50	13.00
*Panorama. Deep orange, shaded mahogany; globular; brilliant		1.25	4.75
Prince of Orange. Terra cotta, edged orange, yellow center	26"	2.50	9.50
Vulcain. Reddish-apricot, margined buff		2.50	9.50
Yellow Perfection. Light bronze-yellow, inside brown	25"	1.15	4.50

Bronze Varieties

	Height	Per 25	Per 100
Abd-El-Kader. Dull bronze-yellow, inside bronzy-brown	26"	2.00	7.50
*Bronze Queen. Soft buff, inside golden-bronze	28"	1.15	4.50
Don Pedro. Coffee-brown; splendid bedder		2.50	9.50
Golden Bronze. Light brownish-yellow, deep mahogany brown with yellow base	24"	1.15	4.50
Goldfinch. Light bronze, inside mahogany; excellent	28"	4.00	15.00
Goder Parfait. Dark violet, white center		2.00	7.50
*Louis XIV. Dark purple; large; globular; wonderful	28"	2.25	8.75
Madras. Golden-bronze, yellow base, starred green	26"	1.10	4.00
Prince Albert. Golden bronze; large formed; green base	32"	2.25	8.75

Lilies

Candidums. Jumbo bulbs	30-31 cm.	12.50	45.00

Japan Lilies

Auratums. White, spotted gold and crimson	11.25	40.00
Speciosum Album. Pure white; large and fine	11.25	40.00
Speciosum Rubrum. White-rayed and spotted crimson	11.25	40.00
Tigrinum Splendens. Orange red, spotted black	7.00	25.00
Tigrinum Flore Pleno. Double Tiger Lily	8.00	30.00
Umbellatum. Various shades of orange and scarlet	7.00	25.00
Regal Lilies. White, spotted crimson. Jumbo bulbs	20.00	75.00
Regal Lilies. Medium to large	11.25	40.00
Regal Lilies. Blooming size	8.00	30.00

Miscellaneous Trees

	Height	Each
Catalpa Bungei. One-year head, 4-foot stem		$2.50
Catalpa Bungei. Three-year head, 6-foot stem		5.00
Teas' Weeping Mulberry. One-year head, 5-foot stem		4.00
Betchel's Double-Flowering Crab.	2-3'	1.50
Betchel's Double-Flowering Crab.	3-4'	3.00
Simonds' Poplar or Lombardy	8-10'	2.00
Simonds' Poplar or Lombardy	10-12'	2.75
Lombardy Poplar or Simonds	5-6'	1.00

Louis XIV Cardinal Manning Yellow Perfection

These eight beautiful varieties of Breeder Tulips, as

Don Pedro
Velvet King

Bronze Queen

Vulcain
Bacchus

illustrated—25 each packed separate—200 Tulips in all, only *$12.50*

CPSIA information can be obtained
at www.ICGtesting.com
Printed in the USA
BVHW051824171218
535791BV00016B/763/P

9 780365 074908